THE LEFT-HANDED BOOK

THE LEFT-HANDED BOOK

BY RAE LINDSAY

FRANKLIN WATTS
New York | London | Toronto | Sydney | 1980
A FIRST BOOK

Photographs courtesy of: United Press International:
pp. 6, 8, 16, 18, 20; The New York Public Library
Picture Collection: pp. 10, 30, 42, 43, 50; Culver Pictures: pp. 12, 34.

Illustration on p. 47 courtesy of *Lefty Magazine*.

Library of Congress Cataloging in Publication Data

Lindsay, Rae.
    The left-handed book.

    (A First book)
    Bibliography: p.
    Includes index.
    SUMMARY: Discusses the history, frequency, and
causes of left-handedness, cites famous people who
are left-handed, and examines the lore about "lefties"
and many of the problems they face.
    1. Left- and right-handedness—Juvenile literature.
[1. Left- and right-handedness] I. Title.
QP385.L56   152.3'35   79–24220
ISBN 0–531–02258–7

CONTENTS

For all the lefties in the world,
and Alex,
my left-handed husband,
and Robbie,
our left-handed boy.

And for Sandy,
who helped with the research,
and Maria,
who helps with everything.

"The King fed himself
with his left hand,
as did we."

James Boswell,
The Life of Johnson,
1791

LEFTIES, UNITE!

Which hand does Jimmy Connors use to volley his way into international tennis championships?

Which hand did strikeout king Sandy Koufax use in pitching fifteen strikeouts in a World Series game against the Yankees?

Which hand does former Beatle and ace musician Paul McCartney use when he plays the guitar?

If you answer left, *right on,* because these famous men are only three of thousands of left-handers who have left their mark on the world. Left-handed people are special because they are different. If Connors, Koufax, and McCartney had been born right-handed, they might never have achieved the fame history has awarded them.

Look around you. Most of your friends, probably your parents and the rest of the family are right-handed. Right-handed people have the world going in their direction. We drive our cars on the right side of the road; when we play baseball, the bases go from right to left; and we paste postage stamps on the right side of the envelope. We dial a telephone with our right hand, take a picture using our right forefinger to click the shutter, turn a doorknob to the right to open a door, and wind our alarm clocks to the right. We read books and write papers from left to right, because that's how books are printed and the way we've been taught to write.

But that wasn't always the case. There was a time, centuries ago, when both hands were equally important, when tools were used with either hand and writing went from *right to left*. In this book we'll be telling you why and when this direction changed.

As it is with so many things in life, though, the majority wins, and the majority of people in this world are right-handed. We lefties, however, are not such a small minority. One researcher, Dr. Bryng Bryngelson of the University of Minnesota, has spent thirty years of his life studying left-handers. He estimates that thirty-five out of every one hundred children born in the world would be lefties if parents or teachers or social customs didn't force them to switch. (And, his research shows that an additional 3 percent would use either hand with equal dexterity).

Even with millions of switchovers, in the United States the actual left-handed population is about 35 million. This figure, composing roughly 15 percent of the population, creeps upward every year, not because more left-handed children are born, but because fewer lefties are being switched or trained to use their right hands. On a worldwide basis, it is estimated that as many as 150 million to 200 million people were born with a predisposition towards being left-handed. (That's almost the total population of the United States.)

In technical terms, lefties are referred to as *sinistrals* (from the Latin, meaning "on the left"), right-handers are called *dextrals* (from the Latin, meaning "on the right"), and people who perform some tasks with one hand and some with the other, or the same tasks with *either* hand, are called *ambidextrals* or *ambidextrous*. This is a confusing misnomer, however, because "ambidextrous" literally means "having *two* right hands."

As we progressed from the primitive life of the cave dwellers to the rich cultures and contributions of ancient Greece and Rome and into what we know as modern times, the gap between left and right became wider and wider. In fact, not only was left or right attributed to handedness, but also to geographic location: some object or place on the right side, or the left side. Superstitions, traditions, and religious customs became associated with the left side or the right side. These ranged from close attention to the direction the sun moves (from left to right if you're facing south) to the famous left-handed handshake of Boy Scouts all over the world.

In the following chapters we will report on these traditions and customs. We will tell you about some of the famous people in history who have been left-handed, either naturally or because of accidents to their right hands, and we will talk about the everyday things that cause most left-handers to perform ambidextrously—like using a scissors.

Thirty years ago, a left-handed child grew up learning to do dozens of ordinary tasks with the right hand—because either this was the way he or she was taught or it was the way most machines and tools worked. Today in the United States, lefties are more widely accepted, and special appliances and tools have been designed just for them. There are even stores that specialize in dozens of left-handed items and books for lefties.

Thomas Carlyle, a famous Scottish historian who was forced to become left-handed after a serious injury to his right hand, said right-handedness is "the very oldest institution that exists." Carlyle lived one hundred years ago (1795–1881). He would be pleased to see that now, in the last quarter of the twentieth century, lefties are gaining their own rights and are making a slow but sure dent in that centuries-old institution.

WELCOME
TO
THE
CLUB

While right-handed people rarely think about which hand another person is using, lefties are quick to spot another southpaw.

There have been some very famous left-handers throughout history who helped shape our world. They include Napoleon and Julius Caesar, Benjamin Franklin and Albert Einstein, Michelangelo and Pablo Picasso, dozens of sports stars and show business greats, and even a skeleton or two in the left-door closet, such as Jack the Ripper and Billy the Kid.

This chapter identifies some celebrities, world champions, and world leaders with whom you share a common bond—lefties all!

WORLD LEADERS

Some of the greatest leaders in history have been lefties, going as far back as the fourth century B.C., when *Alexander the Great*

(356–323 B.C.) of Macedonia conquered the Persian Empire. A few centuries later, *Julius Caesar* (102–44 B.C.) ruled over the entire Roman Empire. Even though he was left-handed, he favored the right-handed handshake and insisted it be used throughout the Empire. By then it was widely believed that anything associated with "right" meant good, while "left" was considered a bad omen.

Another left-handed world leader was *Napoleon,* who was often shown in portraits with his left arm placed slightly behind his back at the waist, a convenient position for drawing his sword. Some historians credit Napoleon with the practice of driving on the left side of the road, still the proper way to drive in Britain. He thought drivers of military transports were safer on the left because the foliage and trees that lined the left side of the road provided some protection from attack. On the left side, too, they could use their sword-bearing right arms to fight any intruders who came from the right.

England boasts some left-handed rulers, too, including *George II,* king from 1727 to 1760, whose tax rates and long-distance governing eventually led to the American Revolution, and *Queen Victoria,* who reigned from 1837 to 1901. Although being left-handed was not encouraged in Victorian days, Victoria's great-great grandson *Prince Charles,* the present heir to the throne, has never been discouraged from favoring his left hand.

Napoleon Bonaparte rode
into the Battle of Wagram
in Austria with a telescope
held firmly in his left *hand.*

In the United States, left-handed leaders have included *James A. Garfield,* twentieth president (1881); *Harry Truman,* thirty-third president (1945–1953); *Gerald Ford,* thirty-eighth president (1974–1977); and Ford's vice-president, *Nelson Rockefeller.*

WRITERS, PHILOSOPHERS, SCIENTISTS

Benjamin Franklin, the talented inventor, writer, and statesman, believed that being left-handed was a disadvantage in a right-handed world. In an essay called "The Left Hand," he wrote:

> *I address myself to all my friends of youth, and conjure them to direct their compassionate regards to my unhappy fate, in order to remove the prejudices of which I am the victim. . . . if by chance I touched a pencil, a pen, or a needle, I was bitterly rebuked; and more than once I have been beaten for being awkward, and wanting a graceful manner.*

Still, Franklin effectively used his left hand to tie the kite in his pioneering study on electricity. He was also the only man to have signed (with his left hand, of course) all four papers relat-

As President of the United States, Gerald Ford in 1974 used his left hand to sign the order of conditional amnesty for Vietnam era draft evaders. Coincidentally, his Vice-President, Nelson Rockefeller, was also left-handed.

ing to the founding of the United States: the Declaration of Independence, the Treaty of Alliance with France, the Treaty of Paris (which ended the Revolutionary War), and the U.S. Constitution.

Another famous left-handed American was Albert Einstein, the Nobel prize-winning physicist and mathematician who modestly declared he only had "two good ideas" in his entire life, one of which was the theory of relativity.

COMPOSERS, MUSICIANS

There are few left-handed classical composers who achieved any degree of fame, possibly because their left-handedness made it difficult to play any instrument except the piano or organ. One was *Carl Philipp Emanuel Bach,* the son of Johann Sebastian Bach. Carl was more famous than his father during his own lifetime. Another classical composer, although right-handed, is a hero to lefties: *Maurice Ravel* wrote a special concerto for the left hand in honor of a pianist friend who had lost his right hand in World War I.

Among modern musicians, the popular folk-rock star *Bob Dylan* is left-handed, and so were fifty percent of the former Beatles, *Paul McCartney* and *Ringo Starr.*

The only left-handed man to sign some of the most important papers concerning the founding of the United States, Benjamin Franklin nonetheless considered his left-handedness a disadvantage in life.

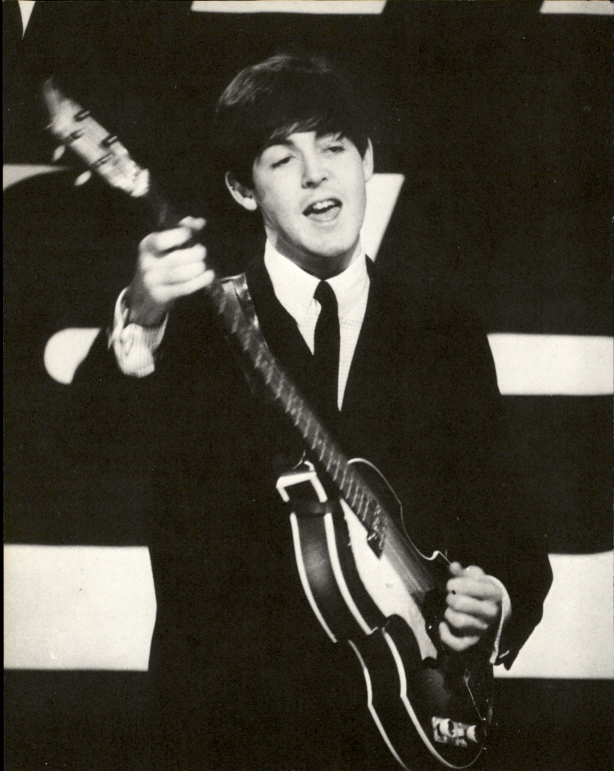

ARTISTS

Leonardo da Vinci (1452–1519) was an Italian creative genius who painted (The Mona Lisa), sculpted, and dreamed up dozens of inventions and ingenious designs ranging from an airplane, a helicopter, and a submarine, to an alarm clock, an oil lamp, and skin-diving equipment—almost five hundred years ago! Leonardo was secretive about his projects: He wrote all his notes from right to left, enabling them to be deciphered only by using a mirror. He, however, was able to read and write in this reverse way *without* a mirror.

Leonardo meant so much to the history of the city of Rome that not only is its airport named after him, but a huge statue of him dominates the airport. He welcomes visitors with a wave of his *left* hand.

An Italian contemporary of Leonardo's was *Michelangelo* (1475–1564), whose renowned works include the decorations for the massive Sistine Chapel at the Vatican, a task which took more than four years to complete. Michelangelo was so versatile he taught himself to use either hand to paint so he could switch when one hand became cramped. If he had been able to use only his left hand, the job might well have taken more than eight years!

Paul McCartney's left-handedness certainly never interfered with his popularity. As a member of the former Beatles, his music appealed to youth all around the world.

13)

SHOW BUSINESS STARS

The entertainment field is well represented by lefties. Among comics were *W. C. Fields;* one of the famous Marx brothers, *Harpo,* who played the harp with his left hand; and *Dick Van Dyke. Carol Burnett* and *Cloris Leachman,* award-winning comediennes/actresses are also left-handed. One of the most famous comic movie stars of all time was *Charlie Chaplin,* whose career as a violinist was frustrated by the problem of reversing the strings on a violin to accommodate his left-handedness.

Danny Kaye, another gifted all-around entertainer, appeared as Papa Gepetto in *Pinocchio* and as Captain Hook in *Peter Pan.* If you look closely at TV reruns, you'll see him wielding his sword in *Peter Pan* and working his puppets in *Pinocchio* with his left hand.

The list of left-handed leading men in films, theater, and TV includes *Peter Fonda,* star of the film *Easy Rider; Paul Michael Glaser,* who shoots left-handed as the Starsky of the TV series *Starsky and Hutch; Michael Landon,* star and director of TV's *Little House on the Prairie;* and *Robert Redford,* noted for the films *The Sting; The Way We Were;* and *All the President's Men.*

As for lefty leading ladies, who could forget the actress and singer *Judy Garland,* best known as Dorothy in the movie *The Wizard of Oz,* or *Marilyn Monroe,* a beautiful blonde who starred in the films *Seven Year Itch, Some Like It Hot,* and *The Misfits.* Film star *Kim Novak* is retired now, but in one of her better movies, *Moll Flanders,* she had to learn to fence with her left hand.

SPORTS FIGURES

Baseball: This is a sport in which lefties really excel. Thirty-two percent of all major league batters, 30 percent of major league pitchers, and 48 percent of big league first basemen are left-handed—but there are no major league left-handed catchers!

The reason left-handed first basemen are in such demand is that a common but difficult play involves a ground ball hit to first base. In this case, the first baseman has to throw to second for the force play and be ready to receive the ball back at first for a double play. This is difficult for a righty, who has to first catch the ball then *turn* his body toward second and throw—a movement which wastes time. A lefty doesn't have to reverse his body position at all.

A right-handed pitcher's curve ball starts at the outside of the plate and curves across the middle of it. To a right-handed batter it seems as if the ball is going to hit him and the batter will "bail out" (step away from the plate)—and have a strike called on him. In this situation, a left-handed batter against a right-handed pitcher is at an advantage because the ball curves *into* his power, and if he connects he can hit a long ball.

The reverse could be true with left-handed pitchers against right-handed batters. However, since most righties don't come up against many lefty pitchers, they are uncomfortable with the direction and curve of the pitch.

As for catchers, the problem for lefties in that position is that when a runner is trying to steal second base, the catcher has to be able to throw to second quickly. Since most batters are right-handed, the left-handed catcher would have to move to the

side before throwing, to avoid hitting the batter. Again, this takes precious time. But as more and more left-handed hitters begin to play ball, the handedness of the catcher will become less crucial. Before long there will undoubtedly be lefty catchers in the major leagues.

Some of the most famous southpaw baseball players are *Vida Blue,* star pitcher for the San Francisco Giants and recipient of the Cy Young Award as Most Valuable Player of 1971; *Ty Cobb,* widely regarded as the greatest player in history and one of the first players elected to the Hall of Fame; *Whitey Ford,* ace pitcher for the New York Yankees during the fifties and sixties; *Reggie Jackson* and *Ron Guidry,* New York Yankees superstars during the 1977 and 1978 World Series; *Sandy Koufax,* the "Man with the Golden Arm," a strikeout king who won twenty-seven games in one season for the Los Angeles Dodgers; *Stan Musial,* who played in over three thousand games with a lifetime .331 average and was National League batting champ seven times; and, of course, *Babe Ruth,* who held the record for lifetime home runs (714) for years and played in more World Series than any other player (ten).

This was the batter's view of Los Angeles Dodger southpaw Sandy Koufax as he made a National League record with 18 strikeouts in one game. The year was 1962, and the Dodgers were playing the Chicago Cubs.

Golf: Left-handed golfers are at an advantage when they play golf *right-handed* because the left arm is really the power arm in the golf swing. So, while it seems as if they are switching to their less powerful arm, this isn't true at all—they are actually capitalizing on their left-handed strength. Another reason most lefties switch to playing golf right-handed is that left-handed clubs are very expensive for a young golfer just starting out. Among the top players in the last ten years, only *Bob Charles* actually plays golf left-handed. *Sam Adams, Ben Hogan,* and *Johnny Miller* are all lefties who play right-handed.

Football: For running backs or defense players there is no advantage or disadvantage to being left-handed. However, a left-handed quarterback, such as former college star *Frankie Albert* or *Kenny Stabler* of the Oakland Raiders, offers the element of surprise to an unsuspecting opposition.

Tennis: This is another great sport for lefties because it confuses right-handed players. A left-handed player is used to playing against righties, but a right-handed opponent must reverse his or her techniques when up against a lefty, and this may prove unsettling. A righty, for example, has to serve to a different area

*In Fenway Park, lefty Reggie Jackson
takes a healthy swing on a strike in
the sixth inning of a Red Sox–Yankee
game in October, 1978. Later on, in
the eighth inning, Jackson connected
for a winning home run for the Yankees,
making them the Eastern Division Champs.*

19)

Presen

of the court to put the ball to a lefty's backhand. Some of the most famous tennis southpaws include *Jimmy Connors*, winner of three U.S. Open Championships; *Rod Laver*, famous Australian player, called "the millionaire of tennis"; *Roscoe Tanner*, an up-and-coming young star; and *Guillermo Vilas*, winner of the 1977 U.S. Open Championship.

Boxing: Left-handed boxers make right-handed ones look awkward because the righties aren't used to dealing with punches coming from the reversed direction. Consequently, it's difficult for lefties to get fights—a situation portrayed so vividly in the movies *Rocky* and *Rocky II* by Sylvester Stallone, who is actually left-handed. But one lefty who succeeded was *James J. Corbett*, heavyweight boxing champion from 1892 to 1897.

Bowling: Although only 15 percent of pro bowlers are lefties, they take in about 60 percent of all the earnings. One reason is that thousands of games are bowled on each bowling alley and since more bowlers are right-handed, the alleys acquire "grooves" on one side. The bowler who is trying to control the ball often finds that it falls into one of these grooves. But the side of the alley is really much "cleaner" for lefties, and they can control the ball better. *Earl Anthony* is probably the best-known pro-

One of the most famous lefty
tennis players, Jimmy Connors
returns the ball during a match
in 1979. Connors cruised to
a 6-1, 6-2 win in the Masters
Grand Prix Tennis Championship.

fessional left-handed bowler; he's won hundreds of thousands of dollars in tournaments.

Miscellaneous Sports: Bruce Jenner is the winner of the 1976 Olympic Decathlon; *Dorothy Hamill* is an Olympic champion skater; *Pélé* helped make soccer a favorite American sport; and *Mark Spitz* is an Olympic champion swimmer.

CRIMINALS

Billy the Kid, the Wild West killer who was actually born in New York, and *The Boston Strangler,* who terrorized Boston during the sixties with more than a dozen murders, were infamous lefties. But even they could not compare with England's notorious *Jack the Ripper,* who was accused of fourteen murders but was never caught. After studying each victim, investigators realized the modus operandi ("way of operating") was similar for every murder. Jack the Ripper would grab his victim from behind, hold her with his right arm, and then use his left hand to slit her throat from right to left. A right-handed person would have cut in the opposite way—from left to right.

DID YOU EVER SEE A LEFT- HANDED CAVEMAN?

Long ago, in the early dawn of civilization, all men and women used whichever hand was most convenient for finding food, climbing hills and mountains, building shelters, and even drawing pictures on the walls of their caves.

Most anthropologists agree that handedness was probably split evenly between lefties and righties thousands of years ago. Artifacts found all over the world prove that Stone Age man (2,000,000–8000 B.C.) made crude instruments which could be used with either hand. Flints, arrowheads, early knives or carving implements were made with double beveling—sharpened edges on both sides—for use with either hand. By the time of the Bronze Age (3500–600 B.C.), however, as tools became more sophisticated, they required hand specialization. And more often than not, the tools that were developed were right-handed tools.

Such tools became prized possessions to be passed on from generation to generation. So, if a man made a tool to be used in the right hand, his children and grandchildren were taught to use that tool with the right hand, whether they had a tendency to be left-handed or not.

As an example, the first sickle for cutting grain or edible grasses was developed in the Bronze Age. It was designed to be used with the right hand, and to this day there is no such thing as a sickle for use with the left hand. So, as people became more and more civilized, the right hand became the "right" hand to use with tools, in customs, and even in language.

The alphabet, however, was a different story. The first alphabet read from right to left and was invented by the Phoenicians, a Mediterranean seafaring tribe which thrived around 3000 to 2000 B.C. As sailors and explorers, they introduced their right-to-left writing to Egypt and Greece. All samples of writing that date back earlier than 600 B.C. move in this right-to-left direction which we know now as "mirror writing." Here is an example of mirror writing:

ʇɟǝl oʇ ʇɥɓᴉɹ ɯoɹɟ ǝʇoɹʍ suɐᴉɔᴉuǝoɥԀ ǝɥꓕ

By about the fifth century B.C., the Greeks began to write from left to right, mainly because of the increasing number of customs and superstitions associated with going in the "right" direction (that is, from left to right). Arab and other Semitic nations, however, continued to read and write from right to left, as they do today. Modern Hebrew and Arabic are only two of several languages referred to as "left-handed tongues." One theory for why these left-handed tongues continue to be used is that they are rooted in religious literature (such as the Bible and Koran), and followers believe it would be sacrilegious to distort or change them in any way.

The ancient Greeks tried to explain handedness and why the right hand should be more dominant. One theory they advanced was related to the center of gravity of the body. They felt that since the liver and lungs were on the right side of the body (they didn't realize we have a *pair* of lungs), people were able to balance better on their left foot. This kept the right hand free for action. In time, they reasoned, the muscles on the right foot and right hand developed more strongly.

Another early theory was that men carried their shields in their left hands to protect the heart, considered then to be on the left side of the body. This made their right hands, which carried weapons, stronger. But then, how did this apply to women, who never carried weapons or shields?

Whatever the theories, by the time the Bible was being written, the right hand was clearly the more important, *good* hand. In the Bible there are more than a hundred positive mentions of the right hand but very few credits for the left. Eve, for example, was created out of Adam's *left* rib, and throughout history, women have been trying to overcome that weak identification and achieve status as equals.

In the New Testament, when Matthew mentions the second coming of the Lord, he says,

He shall separate them one from another, as a shepherd divideth his sheep from the goats and he shall set the sheep on his right *hand, but the goats on his* left. *Then shall the*

King say unto them on his right hand [the sheep], Come, ye blessed of my Father, inherit the Kingdom prepared from the foundations of the world.

There was one group of lefties described in the Old Testament who became notorious. Ironically, they were members of the tribe of Benjamin (*Ben Yamin* literally means "Son of the Right Hand") and were called the "Seven Hundred Slingers," warriors who used slingshots in their left hands. These seven hundred "could sling stones at an hair breadth, and not miss." Their claim to fame was one of terror and warfare, but at the same time, they were described in the Bible as men of courage and valor.

By the time of the Roman Empire (27 B.C.–A.D. 1453), right was "right," and left was left out. Julius Caesar, one of the most famous Roman emperors, was left-handed himself. He decreed that the alphabet would henceforth go from left to right, and that the formal way to greet another Roman was with a right-handed shake.

By now "left-handed" or "left-sided" and "right-handed" and "right-sided" began to take on very special meanings.

WHY ARE SOME OF US LEFT-HANDED?

Aside from superstitions and traditions about handedness, scientists, doctors, and even philosophers have for centuries been trying to explain why some people are left-handed and others right-handed.

Almost 2,500 years ago, Plato, a famous Greek philosopher, believed that the hand that rocks the baby rules which hand the baby will favor. Say, for example, that a baby is always held in its mother's left arm so that the right-handed mother can give the baby a bottle with her right hand. The child will begin to use its own left arm because the right one is tucked next to the mother's body. Since Plato realized this would make most children in the world *left-handed,* he urged mothers to feed and rock their babies holding them in their right arms.

Another theory is based on the idea that we *inherit* the tendency to be left-handed. But this is refuted by the fact that

80 percent of left-handed children are born to right-handed parents. As further proof that the heredity theory doesn't hold up, only one of the famous Dionne quintuplets, born in Canada in 1934, Marie, was left-handed.

Toward the end of the nineteenth century, another early investigator of the left-handed phenomenon, Sir Cyril Burt, found that in 75 percent of the population the bones of the right arm are longer and stronger, but in 9 percent of the population, the left arm is longer and stronger. (The arm strength of the remaining 16 percent of the population is never revealed). But further tests showed that at the time of birth, the length of *both arms* in all babies is identical. The conclusion has to be that the bones and muscles in the "preferred hand"—the hand you use for most things as you grow up—will be better developed by use and skill, not because of birth.

Since 1900 there have been other explanations for handedness: Some people believed that it is related to the rotation of the sun. Others maintained that left-handed children are rebellious and simply insist on using the opposite (left) hand. Still others thought that left-handedness was the result of brain damage. None of these theories stand up under modern experiments.

THE ANSWER LIES IN THE BRAIN

So, scientists turned to the brain itself for an explanation. At first they believed that left-handedness was a genetic (inherited) situation which produces the exact *reverse* effects of being right-handed. But this theory too is refuted, by Dr. Jeannine Herron of the University of California, and herself a lefty, who explains,

"Left-handedness is not a mirror of right-handedness. Left-handers differ in at least two particular ways: they use their non-preferred hand much more often, and may have a different brain organization."

To understand this, we have to take a look at how our brains work. According to Dr. Herron, we don't have one beautifully symmetrical package of gray matter, but two "complementary brains," which work together as a team. Each hemisphere (half) has specific tasks totally different from those of the other.

For most people, the left hemisphere of the brain is the language center and source of logical thinking. It is from the left hemisphere that most people work out math problems, learn chemistry formulas, and learn how to spell words. The right half of the brain usually controls broader concepts, such as your intuitions and your reactions to the five senses. How you see forms and shapes and how you react to sounds and smells are generally controlled from the right half of the brain. The process by which you are able to grasp everything at once, with the result that you get a general impression or feeling from, say, a painting or song, is called "holistic thinking." For most people, holistic thinking originates in the right half of the brain.

The left hemisphere of the brain dictates the movements of the right hand and right side of the body; the right hemisphere moves the left hand, left foot, left side. If our brains and our bodies were all neat and simple, then we would find that right-handers would be the mathematicians, computer experts, and scientists, while lefties would be the artists, the composers, the writers—the creative geniuses.

But it doesn't work out that conveniently. Jeannine Herron points out that both hemispheres are "connected by an enor-

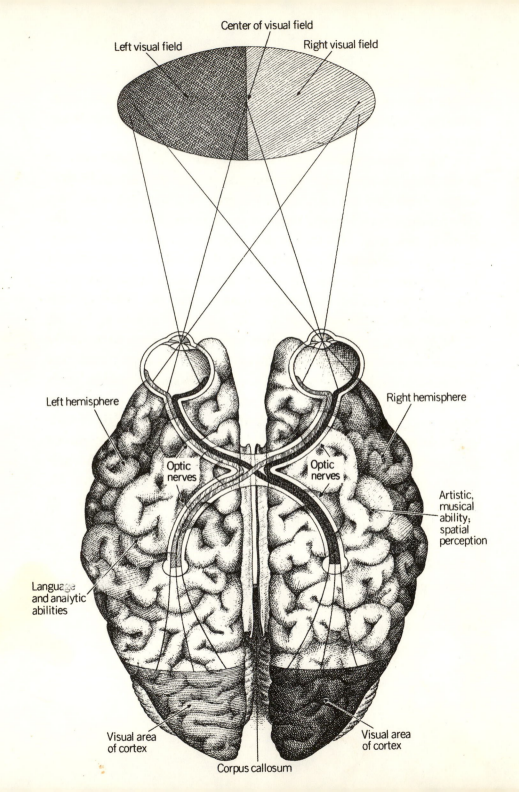

Center of visual field

Left visual field

Right visual field

Left hemisphere

Right hemisphere

Optic nerves

Optic nerves

Artistic, musical ability; spatial perception

Language and analytic abilities

Visual area of cortex

Visual area of cortex

Corpus callosum

mous bundle of fibers called the *corpus callosum,* which allows almost instant communication between the two brain hemispheres. The right hand has access to information in both hemispheres, as does the left."

Still, right-handers generally have their "language center" in the left hemisphere, while only six out of ten lefties process language on the left. The rest of the left-handed population uses either the right side of the brain or both sides. If a dextral (right-handed) person is damaged on the left side of the brain through an accident or illness, he or she usually loses the power of speech. But a sinistral (leftie), who is more likely to utilize both brain hemispheres, can often regain language skill, no matter which half of the brain is injured.

Researcher Jerre Levy of the California Institute of Technology indicates that lefties are superior on verbal problems, but less successful at spatial or perceptual problems. She also believes that lefties who write in the upside-down fashion called "the hook" are the 60 percent with language centers in the left half of the brain, while the 40 percent who write in a mirror image of righties have language centers in the right sphere. We will be talking more about the problems of writing for lefties in the next chapter.

The two hemispheres of the brain
have entirely different functions. The
brain's organization usually dictates
not only which hand you prefer,
but which foot, ear, and eye as well.

In an article in *Science Digest,* another researcher, psychologist Dr. Theodore Blau, observed that southpaws are likely "to be highly imaginative and for some peculiar reason prefer swimming underwater, much more than right-handers."

The brain organization not only dictates which hand you prefer, but also which foot, or eye, or ear. The preference, of course, doesn't actually lie in the hand or the foot or the eye or the ear. It lies in the *brain.* Although nobody ever says. "Wow, you're left-eared," this is part of the same picture as being left-handed. Recent tests, for example, reveal that left-handed people are much more perceptive of changes in musical notes.

The magazine *Scientific American* printed a report in which subjects listened to certain tonal sequences through earphones: One ear received a high tone; the other received a low tone. It was reported that "right-handed subjects tended strongly to hear the high tone in their right ear and the low tone in their left ear and to maintain this percept when the earphones were reversed."

Left-handers, in contrast, "were just as likely to [hear] the high tone in their left ear as in their right." In other words, left-handers tend to be *ambi-aural* (to coin a word) as well as ambidextrous.

HOW MANY LEFTIES ARE THERE?

While current research puts the figure at about fifteen percent of the population, some scientists think that as much as half of humanity would be left-handed if they hadn't been trained to use their right hands as children. The proportion of lefties to righties also varies according to the culture they live in. Clearly, there are more lefties in countries where left-handedness is accepted and fewer in countries like Africa, India, Asia, and the Arab nations, where the left hand is still believed to be the "unclean" hand.

To determine if someone is left-handed or right-handed, researchers very often use the "torque test." All you have to do is draw a circle, first with one hand and then with the other. Lefties and ambidextrals (people who use both hands with ease) draw circles with a clockwise motion. Right-handed people usually make circles in counterclockwise style.

Two problems that occur more often with left-handed and ambidextrous children than with right-handed ones are *stuttering* and *dyslexia*. Dyslexia is a problem involving reading backwards or transposing letters and numbers so that a *6* becomes a *9*, or a *b* becomes a *d*. Dr. Bryng Bryngelson, the Minnesota researcher who studied handedness for thirty years, found that four times as many ambidextrous people rather than true righties were stutterers. One explanation he gives is that since it's more frustrating for lefties or ambidextrals to deal with tools, customs, and other traditions of a right-handed world, this "confuses" the brain and leads to stammering. The situation is even worse when a child is "switched"—forced to use the right hand.

There are many documented cases of the relationship between switched hands and stuttering. King George VI, father of England's Queen Elizabeth II, was switched to writing with his right hand as a child, but he always played tennis and golf skillfully with his *left* hand. Later on in life, he had to have his radio broadcasts taped and then edited to eliminate the stammered words. Another king who was switched as a young child, Louis II of France, became known as Louis the Stammerer.

One man who should have been a lefty and spent his life stammering because of an early switch is Lewis Carroll, author of *Alice's Adventures in Wonderland* and *Through the Looking Glass*. In the Alice books there is always a "duality," a mirror image, which confused Carroll in his own life. Tweedledum and Tweedledee are mirror images of each other. And in *Through the Looking Glass*, everything is reversed. Alice walks *backwards* to meet the Queen; the Red Queen cries *before* she pricks her finger; the White Knight is the one who might "madly squeeze a right-hand foot into a left-hand shoe." (Lefties, who have trouble with directions and in remembering which foot is which, do this all the time). Having been switched troubled Lewis Carroll all his life.

WHEN DO WE BECOME LEFTIES?

Although hand preference first makes its appearance when a child is about six months old, for the next two years any baby will be quite unpredictable as to which hand will dominate. Often a child will use either hand interchangeably for eating, throwing, catching, other everyday tasks. From three to six years,

This sketch of Alice, from Carroll's Through the Looking Glass, *illustrates the duality, or mirror image, which Carroll often used in his stories. At upper left, Alice is shown peering into the looking glass, and at lower right, stepping through the looking glass.*

hand preference becomes firmly established or permanently frustrated. If a right-handed mother insists on giving her child a spoon or fork in his or her right hand, a true lefty may instead grow up to be a confused righty.

Most lefties, however, are ambidextrous to some degree, either through convenience or brain organization or social pressures, and have actually learned to make the best of both worlds.

WHICH IS THE RIGHT MEANING FOR "LEFT"?

Where did the word "left," and other words associated with being left-handed come from? It's interesting to see that the world's major languages have special terms for being left-sided or left-handed, and very few of them are flattering.

LATIN

When you think of how many languages have their origins in Latin, it's clear how far-reaching the influence of the Roman Empire was. There are two Latin word roots which have to do with lefties: the first is *laevus,* an old term for "left hand." The second is *sinister,* which really meant "the pocket side." Pockets in a toga were always on the left, but this didn't come to mean "sinister" as we know it until the Romans adopted the Greek method of predicting events, called "augury."

An augur (a fortune-teller) would stand in a certain direction and then predict coming wars, power struggles, or other major events. In the Greek method of augury, the fortune-tellers faced north and favored the right hand. Anything on the left therefore became sinister, or ominous.

Derivatives of the Latin root *laevus* are seen in some other ancient languages:

MIDDLE AND OLD ENGLISH:
the words are *left* or *lift,* meaning "weak" or "worthless."

OLD GERMAN OR DUTCH:
loof, luchter, lucht, luft, leeft, meaning "weak."

ANGLO SAXON:
lyft, meaning "weak" or "broken."

MODERN LANGUAGES

In MODERN ENGLISH, *The Oxford Dictionary* gives such definitions of left-handed as:

1. Having the left hand more serviceable than the right; using the left hand by preference.
2. (Figuratively) a. crippled, defective; b. awkward, clumsy, inept; c. characterized by underhand dealings.
3. Ambiguous, doubtful, questionable.
4. Ill-omened, sinister.

In the American *Random House Dictionary,* left-handed is defined as "rotating counterclockwise; ambiguous or doubtful as in a left-handed compliment; clumsy or awkward." Centuries ago, when a man of royal ancestry married a commoner, he gave her his left hand instead of his right, therefore denying her certain legal rights.

Here are some other definitions in modern languages: In French, "left" is *gauche,* which also means "awkward" or "clumsy." The Portuguese word for "left," *canhoto,* translates as "weak" or "awkward." In Romany, the word for "left," *bongo,* means "crooked" or "evil." This evil definition of "left" is also seen in Italian, where *mancini* ("left") means "crooked" or even "maimed." In Spanish, *zurdo* not only means "left" but is sometimes also used as an equivalent for *malicioso* ("evil"). *No ser zurdo* means "to be very clever," that is, "*not* to be left-handed."

In addition to the formal meanings and interpretations for "left," "left-handed," or "left-sided," there are slang meanings that are well known. When you're not playing baseball, being "out in left field" means "completely mistaken." A "left-handed compliment" is actually an insult.

In political terms a leftist is someone very liberal, even revolutionary, or a communist. H. L. Mencken, an American journalist who was fascinated by the meanings of words, explained the term "leftist" in his book *The American Language.* Mencken said the word was first introduced by historian Thomas Carlyle in his *French Revolution,* written in 1837. Carlyle described a leftist as someone who sat on the French president's *côté gauche* (left side). These included the radicals, members of the press, and revolutionaries. The aristocrats sat on the president's right, and the moderates sat directly before him.

Because of such meanings (called "colloquialisms"), through the years left-handers have had to cope with the prevailing idea that they must be doing something wrong, certainly not "right."

There are other slang words for left-handers, some good and others bad. In the United States we call a lefty a "southpaw," which comes from the fact that a left-handed pitcher in baseball faces south when he or she winds up to throw the ball. Now the term is used not only for lefties in general, but for all left-handed athletes.

Australians call lefties "molly-dookers," from *molly,* which means "a sissyish man," and *dukes,* slang for "hands." In Northern Ireland, the Protestants call their Catholic rivals "left-footers," an unflattering nickname.

"Left out" means you don't get to play, and "leftovers" are foods nobody wants to eat. When the right hand doesn't know what the left hand is doing, the implication is that the left hand must be doing something wrong.

On the positive side, though, there is one town in America which honors sinistrals: the township of Left Hand, West Virginia, population five hundred.

SUPERSTITIONS, RELIGIONS, AND WIDDERSHINS

By the time of the ancient Romans, the belief that right was good and left was bad began to appear in all areas of human life from religion to superstition.

Some historians theorize that the reason for this was based on the movement of the sun. If you are in the northern hemisphere, and facing south, the sun moves from left to right across the horizon. Because the sun was and is one of the most important symbols of life, the left-to-right movement was considered the only correct direction to go in. The right hand therefore became associated with good and power; the left hand came to represent weakness and evil.

But this theory doesn't hold up if you think of people in the southern hemisphere. Since the sun moves from right to left during the day below the equator, people there would more likely favor the left hand if the sun really determined hand preference.

One of the most famous sun symbols in history has now become an infamous symbol. That is the swastika, which today is always identified with Adolf Hitler and the Nazi party during World War II. But Hitler didn't invent the swastika.

Swastikas showed up all over the world throughout history, in Egypt, Greece, South America, Mexico, Britain, Ireland, Spain, India, and North America. The hooks on a swastika follow the left-to-right direction of the sun's movement and therefore represented good luck or good fortune.

There is another kind of swastika, however, that was considered a good luck sign by a left-handed sect that lived at one time in southern India. This swastika, with a right-to-left movement, was adapted as a favorable omen by Rudyard Kipling, an author of many books about India. In fact, many of his books were decorated with the sign.

The idea that moving counterclockwise was not only contrary, but downright evil is found in the Scottish concept of "widdershins," a derivation of the German word *Wiederschein,* meaning "against the sun." The Scots believed that devils and witches ran counter to the sun. So, if a person walked or ran widdershins, he or she was thought to like the devil and perhaps even be a witch.

People were accused of witchcraft for such simple actions

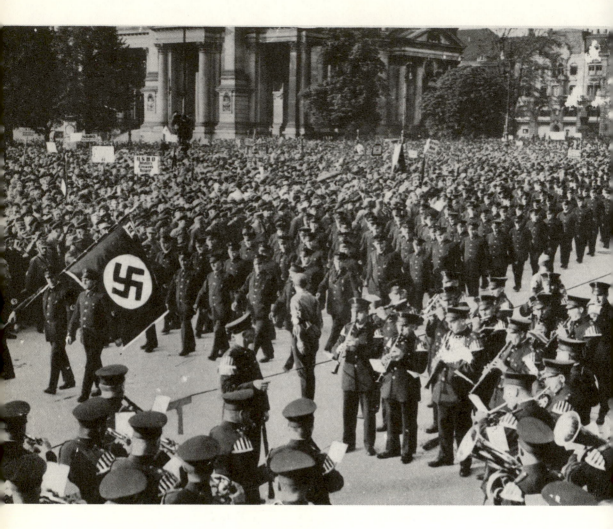

Adolf Hitler used the swastika as a symbol of the Nazi Party in Germany during the 1930s and early 1940s. Up until that point, it had been used primarily as a symbol of good fortune.

The Hopi Indians, an American tribe, used this dance rattle to bring them good luck. In the center of the rattle is a swastika with a left to right movement.

as walking around a barn from the right to the left instead of from left to right. At the Salem witch trials in New England in the seventeenth century, widdershin movements were used as evidence, but matters were made even worse if the accused witch was left-handed as well!

In France, several centuries earlier, Joan of Arc was burned as a witch, even though she is now considered a saint in the Catholic Church. She came from the region of Lorraine, where people believed in the power of witchcraft and the devil. Sketches of the time show Joan carrying her sword in her *left* hand.

In many paintings and drawings the devil himself is depicted as being left-handed. A French superstition is that Satan greets witches and is greeted by them *avec le bras gauche,* "with the left arm."

This association of the left side with the devil is still recognized in as common a custom as throwing a little salt over your left shoulder—in other words, in the devil's direction—if you spill salt at the table. The origin of this superstition is that at the Last Supper, before Jesus Christ was turned over to Pilate for his crucifixion, Judas, the apostle who betrayed Christ, spilled the salt.

The emphasis on left and right shows up in other religions as well. Orthodox Jews wear "phylacteries"—leather boxes containing Hebrew texts—attached to their left hands.

Buddhists believe in two very important symbols: the Yang and the Yin. The Yang is active, male, represents light, life, and the right hand; the Yin is passive, female, earth, darkness, and the left hand. But when the two symbols are united in a circle, it becomes a symbol of harmony, something the Chinese call "the Tao."

BEST FOOT FORWARD

The left foot plays its part in superstitions, too. In Roman times it was thought to be unlucky to enter a house with the left foot first. This practice was adopted by the Scots in a tradition called "first footing," which they still follow on Hogmanay (New Year's Eve). To enter a house with the left foot first would bring bad luck to the occupants for the new year ahead.

However, soldiers always march with the left foot first in a left-right, left-right pattern. One theory as to why the left-foot-first movement is preferred for marching is that the left leg is weaker, so that any injury incurred isn't as serious. Another explanation is that since the right arm holds the weapon, a left-foot-forward movement will give momentum for the right hand.

One left-foot superstition is lucky for human beings, but not so lucky for rabbits. During early days in America, a rabbit was always on hand whenever someone was executed. The animal's left hind leg was cut off and given to the executioner to protect him from misfortune. This is how the rabbit's foot became a common good luck charm.

IS IT EASIER TO SWITCH THAN FIGHT?

If you're left-handed, there are dozens of things you have to learn to do with your right hand. But the most difficult task all of us lefties have to learn to do is to write with our *left* hand.

I have never met a lefty who got an A in penmanship. The best I could ever manage was a C. My teachers always insisted that we slant our papers to the left, which, of course is correct for righties but not for lefties. I very stubbornly would switch my paper to the right, which made it much easier for me to write somewhat legibly.

About 60 percent of left-handed children do slant their papers to the left, as instructed, and therefore write in the upside-down position known as "the hook," in which the writing is actually done from *above* the line. For those of us lefties who slant to the right and write in the same fashion as righties (with the hand positioned *below* the line), our work is often sloppy because as we write we tend to smear the words already completed.

46)

Here's how both types of lefties write:

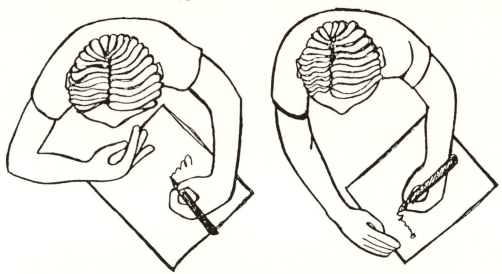

But aside from neatness, the act of writing itself is physically tiring for lefties. A right-handed boy or girl, working from left to right, is actually *pulling* the pen—the pen moves naturally across the page. But lefties could well be called "pen pushers." They have to push the pen or pencil along. Because their hands get tired of pushing, they tend to write more laboriously and more carefully than righties.

It's interesting that left-handed signatures, written so carefully and painstakingly, are notoriously easy for forgers to imitate. Another factor is that lefties tend to have several variations of their signatures, depending on how tired they are or how much they've already written. In fact, their signatures vary more than the signatures of right-handers.

Although lefties and their left-handed writing are more and more accepted in America, England, France, Sweden, and other industrialized countries, left-handed writing is still frowned upon in such countries as Greece, Russia, and most Arab countries. Still, when children are forced to use their right hands when the preferred hand is the left, the result is often undecipherable.

There have been cases where right-handed people, because of an injury, had to learn to write with their left hands. One of the most famous is Lord Nelson, an English naval hero, who lost the use of his right hand in a battle. At first his left-handed writing was awkward, clumsy, and almost illegible. But many years later, after decades of practice, his left-handed writing was as beautiful and precise as his original right-handed script had been.

WORD GAMES LEFTIES PLAY

While there are problems that arise from working left to right when you'd rather go the other way, there are also interesting word games at which lefties seem to excel. These seem to be the result of the confusion that sometimes arises because lefties are more likely to process information from both sides of the brain. One of these games is called a *spoonerism,* named after Dr. Spooner of Oxford University in England. Dr. Spooner not only mixed up *b*'s and *p*'s and *6*'s and *9*'s, but he frequently transposed letters and words so that

Conquering Kings became *Kingering Congs*
or

Let us have flags hung from the window in his honor
became

Let us have hags flung from the window in his honor.

His research showed that lefties are more likely than right-ies to mix up sentences like this. Most left-handers are also fas-cinated by *palindromes,* which are phrases or sentences that can be read backwards or forwards. Some classic examples:

Draw pupil's lip upward. Read that from right to left and you'll see it says exactly the same thing.

Another is:

A man, a plan, a canal—panama!

One of my all-time favorite palindromes is one that might have been said by the first man to his mate:

"Madam, I'm Adam."

Her reply, of course, was, *"Eve."*

Some of the first words left-handed (and right-handed) children learn to spell are palindromes. They include: mom, pop, dad, sis, toot, pep, pop, bob. Can you think of some others?

MAKING MUSIC LEFT-HANDED

Although the piano or such instruments as the clarinet or sax-ophone must be played with both hands (there is no such thing as a left-handed saxophone), stringed instruments—the guitar, violin, mandolin, banjo—pose problems for a lefty. The strings must actually be reversed. Charlie Chaplin, who composed most of the music for his films, wrote in his life story *My Autobiography*: "Since the age of sixteen I had practiced from four to six hours a day in my bedroom. . . . as I played left-handed, my violin was strung left-handed with the bass bar and sounding post reversed. I had great ambitions to be a concert

artist. . . . but as time went by I realized I could not achieve excellence, so I gave it up."

In the classic 1952 movie *Limelight*, Chaplin is featured playing his violin "widdershins." But can you imagine how a left-handed violinist would look in a symphony orchestra where the bows of nineteen violinists are going in one direction and the bow of a left-handed musician is moving in the opposite direction?

LEFTIES ARE FLEXIBLE

Because so many objects and appliances are designed for use by righties, lefties have learned to adjust. Eating is one of the most common examples of this flexibility. Most lefties will use a knife with their right hand and the fork with their left. They don't have to bother to switch the fork to their other hand as so many righties do. Actually, this is a much more graceful method of eating than the constant switching of right-handers. It's also the common practice—no matter which hand is preferred—in Europe. But of course when a left-handed person is using a knife alone—let's say when cutting cheese or peeling a piece of fruit—the knife is held firmly in the *left* hand.

One modern convenience that seems to favor the left is the

Lefty Charlie Chaplin, who once had great ambitions to be a concert violinist, is shown here in the movie The Vagabond *playing the violin "widdershins."*

telephone. Although it was designed for dialing and depositing coins with the right hand, the receiver is usually held to the left ear, a lefty's "better" ear. The only difficulty for lefties when using the phone is that if you're holding the phone to your left ear with your left hand and want to write down a message, you have to scrunch the phone between your ear and your shoulder to leave your writing hand free. If you try to listen with your right ear, the wire gets in your way.

So, lefties learn to perform ambidextrously. They learn to turn right to open doors, lock windows, close suitcases, use keys, wind clocks, sharpen a pencil, turn on the hot water, start a car, use an adding machine or calculator, work a vacuum cleaner, or play a record. If you are cooking, you have to be *adroit* (graceful with the right hand) at tilting some appliances with your right hand because the pouring lip is set up for righties. Of course, you can also tip it *backwards* with your left.

In your parents' car you'll notice that everything of importance is on the right: the ignition switch, the gear shift, the radio, the lighter, the ashtray. The accelerator and brake, of course, are worked with the right foot, even though you, lefty, are probably left-footed.

Even typewriters, are geared for right-handed typists. The most significant keys are on the right, including the on-off button, the carriage return and back space, the period, comma, and those essential quotation and exclamation marks.

There are also some manual projects that are very difficult for lefties to learn. Knitting, crocheting, and embroidery, for example, all pose problems, because the instruction booklets are written for right-handers.

It's no wonder we lefties get confused.

Once you're established as a lefty or righty, you do certain tasks with certain hands, and it's difficult to switch unless you are forced to. There are some "ambi" sports stars in tennis, golf, baseball, who *can* switch-hit, however, and this throws their opponents into confusion. (It's about time somebody else was confused!)

RIGHT ON FOR LEFTIES

We lefties have come a long way in the years since I was a child. Today, if you choose to write with your left hand, in most schools you'll be encouraged, not switched. Left-handed scissors are common in kindergarten and early elementary grades—all you have to do is ask for them. If you request the outside left-hand place setting at a table, the hostess or your dinner partners will realize this makes dining easier for everybody, not just you. (You won't be banging elbows with the person next to you.)

And today, there are many more sources and products to help a left-handed person function in a right-handed world. Now you can buy a left-handed iron or scissors in most hardware stores. There are books that teach you how to do needlepoint or play golf left-handed, left-handed bowling gloves, and even left-handed grapefruit knives.

There are at least a dozen stores specializing in products for southpaws, devices and tools and equipment you never dreamed were available. Some of the most unusual items include:

- A device to attach to the gear shift on a car so that you can shift gears with your left hand.
- A left-foot accelerator for cars.
- A left-handed ruler with numbers beginning at the right.
- A left-handed power saw.
- A thermometer that you can read while holding it in your left hand.
- Left-handed playing cards with numbers in all four corners so you can fan cards in either direction.
- Guitars strung for lefties.
- Archery sets strung for lefties.
- Left-handed golf clubs, baseball gloves, even a boomerang.
- Left-handed diaper pins.
- Left-handed can openers, mixing tools, vegetable parers, ice cream scoops.
- Cameras with shutters on the left.
- Watches that wind to the left, on the left-hand side.

Among my favorite purchases at "The Left Hand," a store in New York City, was a T-shirt imprinted "Lefties of the World Unite," and a giant button that reads "Kiss Me, I'm Left-Handed."

I've always liked being left-handed; it made me feel different and special. And I've found that left-handed people have a kindred spirit of affection and appreciation for other lefties. It's as if we belong to our own unique club. You don't have to pay any dues to belong to this club, and you don't even have to learn a "Bill of Lefts." But you do share membership with some world-famous, very talented men and women. To be a member in good standing all you have to do is proudly use your good *left* hand!

54)

SHOPS, SOURCES, CLUBS FOR SOUTHPAWS

CLUBS

League of Lefthanders
Mr. Bob Geden
P.O. Box 89
New Milford, New Jersey 07646

Left-Handers,
International
Ms. Jancy Campbell
Executive Director
3601 S.W. 29th Street
Topeka, Kansas 66614

STORES SELLING
LEFT-HANDED MERCHANDISE

United States

Left-Hand World of Carmel, Inc.
Vandervort Court (San Carlos at 7th)
Mailing Address:
P.O. Box 7222
Carmel-by-the-Sea, California 93921

The Left-Handed Complement
11359 Bolas Street
Los Angeles, California 90049

Lefty, Inc.
P.O. Box 1054
Torrence, California 90505

The Lefty Shop
7008 S. Washington Avenue
Whittier, California 90602

The Aristera Organization
9 Rice's Lane, P.O. Box 647
Westport, Connecticut 06880

Lefthand Plus, Inc.
P.O. Box 161
Morton Grove, Illinois 60053

Left Handed Complements
P.O. Box 647
Brookline Village, Massachusetts 02147

The Left Hand
140 West 22nd Street
New York, N.Y. 10011

The Southpaw
5331 S.W. Macadam Avenue
Portland, Oregon 97201

The Southpaw
12215 Cot Road
Dallas, Texas 75251

Left-Handed Limited
433 W. Silver Spring Drive
Milwaukee, Wisconsin 53217

Stores in Other Countries

Lefthanded Products
Box 5189, G.P.O. Sydney, N.S.W. 2001
Sydney, Australia

The Left-Hander
P.O. Box 211, N.D.G. Station
Montreal, Quebec, Canada H4A 3P5

Anything Left-Handed, Ltd.
65 Beak Street, P.O. Box 4SL
London, England WIA 45SL

The Sinister Shop
749 Queen Street. W.
Toronto, Ontario, Canada, M6J 1G1

FOR FURTHER READING

GENERAL BOOKS

Barsley, Michael. *Left-Handed People*. Hollywood, Calif.: Wilshire Book Co., 1976.

DeKay, James T. *The Left Handed Book*. Philadelphia: J. B. Lippincott Co. 1966.

Fincher, Jack. *Sinister People: The Looking-Glass World of the Left-Hander*. New York: G. P. Putnam & Sons, 1977.

Lerner, Marguerite R. *Lefty*. Minneapolis: Lerner Publication Co., 1960.

CRAFTS, HOBBIES, SPORTS

Charles, Bob. *Lefthanded Golf*. Englewood Cliffs, N.J.: Prentice Hall, 1965.

Clarke, Nicholas. *Guitar Instructions for Left-Handed Guitar.* New York: The Left Hand, 140 W. 22 Street, New York, N.Y. 10011, n.d.

Myers, Carole R. *A Primer of Left-Handed Embroidery.* New York: Scribner, 1974.

Slater, Elaine. *The New York Times Book of Needlepoint for Left-Handers.* New York: Quadrangle, 1974.

Schwed, Peter. *Sinister Tennis: How to Play Against and With Left Handers.* New York: Doubleday, 1975.

Note: In addition to these books, many of the stores mentioned earlier carry special pamphlets and specially published books for lefties which cannot be found in libraries or bookstores. The store catalogs list these books.

INDEX

63)

ABOUT THE AUTHOR

Rae Lindsay is a nationally syndicated columnist whose "First Person Singular" column is distributed by the Associated Press to over forty newspapers across the country. She is the author of ten books for adults, and her articles on lifestyles have appeared widely in magazines. Also the author of *Sleep and Dreams,* published by Franklin Watts, this is her second book for young adults.

Rae Lindsay lives with her three children in northern New Jersey where she works as a free-lance writer.